The Real
Inspector Hound

The Real Inspector Hound

TOM STOPPARD

Grove Press, Inc.
New York

The first performance of *The Real Inspector Hound* was given on June 17, 1968, at the Criterion Theatre, London. It was directed by Robert Chetwyn and designed by Hutchinson Scott. The cast was as follows:

MOON	Richard Briers
BIRDBOOT	Ronnie Barker
MRS. DRUDGE	Josephine Tewson
SIMON	Robin Ellis
FELICITY	Patricia Shakesby
CYNTHIA	Caroline Blakiston
MAGNUS	Antony Webb
INSPECTOR HOUND	Hugh Walters

The first thing is that the audience appear to be confronted by their own reflection in a huge mirror. Impossible. However, back there in the gloom—not at the footlights—a bank of plush seats and pale smudges of faces. The total effect having been established, it can be progressively faded out as the play goes on, until the front row remains to remind us of the rest and then, finally, merely two seats in that row—one of which is now occupied by MOON. *Between* MOON *and the auditorium is an acting area which represents, in as realistic an idiom as possible, the drawing-room of Muldoon Manor. French windows at one side. A telephone fairly well upstage (i.e. towards* MOON). *The body of a man lies sprawled face down on the floor in front of a large settee. This settee must be of a size and design to allow it to be wheeled over the body, hiding it completely. Silence. The room. The body.* MOON.*

MOON stares blankly ahead. He turns his head to one side then the other, then up, then down—waiting. He picks up his programme and reads the front cover. He turns over the page and reads.

He turns over the page and reads.
He turns over the page and reads.
He turns over the page and reads.
He looks at the back cover and reads.
He puts it down, crosses his legs, and looks about. He stares front. Behind him and to one side, barely visible, a man enters and sits down: BIRDBOOT.

Pause. MOON *picks up his programme, glances at the front cover and puts it down impatiently. Pause. . . . Behind him there is the crackle of a chocolate-box, absurdly loud.* MOON *looks round. He and* BIRDBOOT *see each other. They are clearly known to each other. They acknowledge each other with constrained waves.* MOON *looks straight ahead.* BIRDBOOT *comes down to join him.*

Note: Almost always, MOON *and* BIRDBOOT *converse in tones suitable for an auditorium, sometimes a whisper. However good the acoustics might be, they will have to have microphones where they are sitting. The effect must be not of sound picked up, amplified and flung out at the audience, but of sound picked up, carried and gently dispersed around the auditorium.*

Anyway, BIRDBOOT, *with a box of Black Magic chocolates, makes his way down to join* MOON *and plumps himself down next to him, plumpish, middle-aged* BIRDBOOT *and younger, taller, less-relaxed* MOON.

BIRDBOOT (*sitting down; conspiratorially*): Me and the lads have had a meeting in the bar and decided it's first-class family entertainment but if it goes on beyond half-past ten it's self-indulgent—pass it on . . . (*and laughs jovially.*) I'm on my own tonight, don't mind if I join you?

MOON: Hello, Birdboot.

BIRDBOOT: Where's Higgs?

MOON: I'm standing in.

MOON *and* BIRDBOOT: Where's Higgs?

MOON: Every time.

BIRDBOOT: What?

8

MOON: It is as if we only existed one at a time, combining to achieve continuity. I keep space warm for Higgs. My presence defines his absence, his absence confirms my presence, his presence precludes mine. . . . When Higgs and I walk down this aisle together to claim our common seat, the oceans will fall into the sky and the trees will hang with fishes.

BIRDBOOT (*he has not been paying attention, looking around vaguely, now catches up*): Where's Higgs?

MOON: The very sight of me with a complimentary ticket is enough. The streets are impassable tonight, the country is rising and the cry goes up from hill to hill—Where—is—Higgs? (*Small pause.*) Perhaps he's dead at last, or trapped in a lift somewhere, or succumbed to amnesia, wandering the land with his turn-ups stuffed with ticket-stubs.

BIRDBOOT *regards him doubtfully for a moment.*

BIRDBOOT: Yes . . . Yes, well I didn't bring Myrtle tonight—not exactly her cup of tea, I thought, tonight.

MOON: Over her head, you mean?

BIRDBOOT: Well, no—I mean it's a sort of a *thriller*, isn't it?

MOON: Is it?

BIRDBOOT: That's what I heard. Who-killed thing?—no-one-will-leave-the-house?

MOON: I suppose so. Underneath.

BIRDBOOT: *Underneath?!?* It's a whodunnit, man!—Look at it!

They look at it. The room. The body. Silence.

Has it started yet?

9

MOON: Yes.

Pause. They look at it.

BIRDBOOT: Are you sure?

MOON: It's a pause.

BIRDBOOT: You can't start with a *pause!* If you want my opinion there's total panic back there. (*Laughs and subsides.*) Where's Higgs tonight, then?

MOON: It will follow me to the grave and become my epitaph—Here lies Moon the second string: where's Higgs? . . . Sometimes I dream of revolution, a bloody *coup d'état* by the second rank—troupes of actors slaughtered by their understudies, magicians sawn in half by indefatigably smiling glamour girls, cricket teams wiped out by marauding bands of twelfth men—I dream of champions chopped down by rabbit-punching sparring partners while eternal bridesmaids turn and rape the bridegrooms over the sausage rolls and parliamentary private secretaries plant bombs in the Minister's Humber—comedians die on provincial stages, robbed of their feeds by mutely triumphant stooges—And march—an army of assistants and deputies, the seconds-in-command, the runners-up, the right-hand men—storming the palace gates wherein the second son has already mounted the throne having committed regicide with a croquet mallet—stand-ins of the world stand up!—

Beat.

Sometimes I dream of Higgs.

Pause. BIRDBOOT *regards him doubtfully. He is at a loss, and grasps reality in the form of his box of chocolates.*

10

BIRDBOOT (*chewing into mike*): Have a chocolate!

MOON: What kind?

BIRDBOOT (*chewing into mike*): Black Magic.

MOON: No thanks.

Chewing stops dead.
Of such tiny victories and defeats . . .

BIRDBOOT: I'll give you a tip, then. Watch the girl.

MOON: You think she did it?

BIRDBOOT: No, no—the *girl*, watch her.

MOON: What girl?

BIRDBOOT: You won't know her. I'll give you a nudge.

MOON: *You* know her, do you?

BIRDBOOT (*suspiciously, bridling*): What's *that* supposed to mean?

MOON: I beg your pardon?

BIRDBOOT: I'm trying to tip you a wink—give you a nudge as good as a tip—for God's sake, Moon, what's the matter with you?—you could do yourself some good, spotting her first time out—she's new, from the provinces, going straight to the top. I don't want to put words into your mouth but a word from us and we could make her.

MOON: I suppose you've made dozens of them, like that.

BIRDBOOT (*instantly outraged*): I'll have you know I'm a family man devoted to my homely but good-natured wife, and if you're suggesting—

MOON: No, no—

BIRDBOOT: —A man of my scrupulous morality—

MOON: I'm sorry—

BIRDBOOT: —falsely besmirched—

MOON: Is that her?

For MRS. DRUDGE *has entered.*

11

BIRDBOOT: —don't be absurd, wouldn't be seen dead with the old—ah.

MRS. DRUDGE is the char, middle-aged, turbanned. She heads straight for the radio, dusting on the trot.

MOON (*reading his programme*): Mrs. Drudge the Help.

RADIO (*without preamble, having been switched on by* MRS. DRUDGE): We interrupt our programme for a special police message.

MRS. DRUDGE stops to listen.

The search still goes on for the escaped madman who is on the run in Essex.

MRS. DRUDGE (*fear and dismay*): Essex!

RADIO: County police led by Inspector Hound have received a report that the man has been seen in the desolate marshes around Muldoon Manor.

Fearful gasp from MRS. DRUDGE.

The man is wearing a darkish suit with a lightish shirt. He is of medium height and build and youngish. Anyone seeing a man answering to this description and acting suspiciously, is advised to phone the nearest police station.

A man answering this description has appeared behind MRS. DRUDGE. *He is acting suspiciously. He creeps in. He creeps out.* MRS. DRUDGE *does not see him. He does not see the body.*

That is the end of the police message.

12

MRS. DRUDGE *turns off the radio and resumes her cleaning. She does not see the body. Quite fortuitously, her view of the body is always blocked, and when it isn't she has her back to it. However, she is dusting and polishing her way towards it.*

BIRDBOOT: So that's what they say about me, is it?

MOON: What?

BIRDBOOT: Oh, I know what goes on behind my back—sniggers—slanders—hole-in-corner innuendo—What have you heard?

MOON: Nothing.

BIRDBOOT (*urbanely*): Tittle tattle. Tittle, my dear fellow, tattle. I take no notice of it—the sly envy of scandal mongers—I can afford to ignore them, I'm a respectable married man—

MOON: Incidentally—

BIRDBOOT: Water off a duck's back, I assure you.

MOON: Who was that lady I saw you with last night?

BIRDBOOT (*unexpectedly stung into fury*): How dare you! (*More quietly.*) How dare you. Don't you come here with your slimy insinuations! My wife Myrtle understands perfectly well that a man of my critical standing is obliged occasionally to mingle with the world of the footlights, simply by way of keeping *au fait* with the latest—

MOON: I'm sorry—

BIRDBOOT: That a critic of my scrupulous integrity should be vilified and pilloried in the stocks of common gossip—

MOON: Ssssh—

BIRDBOOT: I have nothing to hide!—why, if this should reach the ears of my beloved Myrtle—

13

MOON: Can I have a chocolate?

BIRDBOOT: What? Oh—(*Mollified.*) Oh yes—my dear fellow—yes, let's have a chocolate—No point in—yes, good show. (*Pops chocolate into his mouth and chews.*) Which one do you fancy?—Cherry? Strawberry? Coffee cream? Turkish delight?

MOON: I'll have montelimar.

Chewing stops.

BIRDBOOT: Ah. Sorry. (*Just missed that one.*)

MOON: Gooseberry fondue?

BIRDBOOT: No.

MOON: Pistacchio fudge? Nectarine cluster? Hickory nut praline? Château Neuf du Pape '55 cracknell?

BIRDBOOT: I'm afraid not. . . . Caramel?

MOON: Yes, all right.

BIRDBOOT: Thanks very much. (*He gives* MOON *a chocolate. Pause.*) Incidentally, old chap, I'd be grateful if you didn't mention—I mean, you know how these misunderstandings get about. . . .

MOON: What?

BIRDBOOT: The fact is, Myrtle simply doesn't *like* the theatre . . . (*He trails off hopelessly.*)

MRS. DRUDGE, *whose discovery of the body has been imminent, now—by way of tidying the room —slides the couch over the corpse, hiding it completely. She resumes dusting and humming.*

MOON: By the way, congratulations, Birdboot.

BIRDBOOT: What?

MOON: At the Theatre Royal. Your entire review reproduced in neon!

BIRDBOOT (*pleased*): Oh . . . that old thing.

14

MOON: You've seen it, of course.

BIRDBOOT (*vaguely*): Well, I was passing. . . .

MOON: I definitely intend to take a second look when it has settled down.

BIRDBOOT: As a matter of fact I have a few colour transparencies—I don't know whether you'd care to . . ?

MOON: Please, please—love to, love to . . .

BIRDBOOT hands over a few colour slides and a battery-powered viewer which MOON *holds up to his eyes as he speaks.*

Yes . . . yes . . . lovely . . . awfully sound. It has scale, it has colour, it is, in the best sense of the word, electric. Large as it is, it is a small masterpiece—I would go so far as to say—kinetic without being pop, and having said that, I think it must be said that here we have a review that adds a new dimension to the critical scene. I urge you to make haste to the Theatre Royal, for this is the stuff of life itself. (*Handing back the slides, morosely.*) All I ever got was "Unforgettable" on the posters for . . . What was it?

BIRDBOOT: Oh—yes— I know . . . Was that you? I thought it was Higgs.

The phone rings. MRS. DRUDGE *seems to have been waiting for it to do so and for the last few seconds has been dusting it with an intense concentration. She snatches it up.*

MRS. DRUDGE (*into phone*): Hello, the drawing-room of Lady Muldoon's country residence one morning in early spring? . . . He*llo!*—the draw—Who? Whom did you wish to speak to? I'm afraid there is no one

15

of that name here, this is all very mysterious and I'm sure it's leading up to something, I hope nothing is amiss for we, that is Lady Muldoon and her houseguests, are here cut off from the world, including Magnus, the wheelchair-ridden half-brother of her ladyship's husband Lord Albert Muldoon who ten years ago went out for a walk on the cliffs and was never seen again.

MOON: Derivative, of course.

BIRDBOOT: But quite sound.

MRS. DRUDGE: Should a stranger enter our midst, which I very much doubt, I will tell him you called. Good-bye.

She puts down the phone and catches sight of the previously seen suspicious character who has now entered again, more suspiciously than ever, through the French windows. He senses her stare, freezes, and straightens up.

SIMON: Ah!—hello there! I'm Simon Gascoyne, I hope you don't mind, the door was open so I wandered in. I'm a friend of Lady Muldoon, the lady of the house, having made her acquaintance through a mutual friend, Felicity Cunningham, shortly after moving into this neighbourhood just the other day.

MRS. DRUDGE: I'm Mrs. Drudge. I don't live in but I pop in on my bicycle when the weather allows to help in the running of charming though somewhat isolated Muldoon Manor. Judging by the time (*she glances at the clock*) you did well to get here before high water cut us off for all practical purposes from the outside world.

SIMON: I took the short cut over the cliffs and followed

16

one of the old smugglers' paths through the treacherous swamps that surround this strangely inaccessible house.

MRS. DRUDGE: Yes, many visitors have remarked on the topographical quirk in the local strata whereby there are no roads leading from the Manor, though there *are* ways of getting *to* it, weather allowing.

SIMON: Yes, well I must say it's a lovely day so far.

MRS. DRUDGE: Ah, but now that the cuckoo-beard is in bud there'll be fog before the sun hits Foster's Ridge.

SIMON: I say, it's wonderful how you country people really know weather.

MRS. DRUDGE (*suspiciously*): Know whether what?

SIMON (*glancing out of the window*): Yes, it does seem to be coming on a bit foggy.

MRS. DRUDGE: The fog is very treacherous around here— it rolls off the sea without warning, shrouding the cliffs in a deadly mantle of blind man's buff.

SIMON: Yes, I've heard it said.

MRS. DRUDGE: I've known whole week-ends when Muldoon Manor, as this lovely old Queen Anne House is called, might as well have been floating on the pack ice for all the good it would have done phoning the police. It was on such a week-end as this that Lord Muldoon who had lately brought his beautiful bride back to the home of his ancestors, walked out of this house ten years ago, and his body was never found.

SIMON: Yes indeed, poor Cynthia.

MRS. DRUDGE: His name was Albert.

SIMON: Yes indeed, poor Albert. But tell me, is Lady Muldoon about?

17

MRS. DRUDGE: I believe she is playing tennis on the lawn with Felicity Cunningham.

SIMON (*startled*): Felicity Cunningham?

MRS. DRUDGE: A mutual friend, I believe you said. A happy chance. I will tell them you are here.

SIMON: Well, I can't really stay as a matter of fact— please don't disturb them—I really should be off.

MRS. DRUDGE: They would be very disappointed. It is some time since we have had a four for pontoon bridge at the Manor, and I don't play cards myself.

SIMON: There is another guest, then?

MRS. DRUDGE: Major Magnus, the crippled half-brother of Lord Muldoon who turned up out of the blue from Canada just the other day, completes the house-party.

MRS. DRUDGE *leaves on this.* SIMON *is undecided.*

MOON (*ruminating quietly*): I think I must be waiting for Higgs to die.

BIRDBOOT: What?

MOON: Half-afraid that I will vanish when he does.

The phone rings. SIMON *picks it up.*

SIMON: Hello?

MOON: I wonder if it's the same for Puckeridge?

BIRDBOOT *and* SIMON (*together*): Who?

MOON: Third string.

BIRDBOOT: Your stand-in?

MOON: Does he wait for Higgs and I to write each other's obituary—does he dream—?

SIMON: To whom did you wish to speak?

BIRDBOOT: What's he like?

MOON: Bitter.

SIMON: There is no one of that name here.

BIRDBOOT: No—as a critic, what's Puckeridge like as a critic?

MOON (*laughs poisonously*): Nobody knows—

SIMON: You must have got the wrong number!

MOON: —There's always been me and Higgs.

SIMON *replaces the phone and paces nervously. Pause.* BIRDBOOT *consults his programme.*

BIRDBOOT: Simon Gascoyne. It's not him, of course.

MOON: What?

BIRDBOOT: I said it's not him.

MOON: Who is it, then?

BIRDBOOT: My guess is Magnus.

MOON: In disguise, you mean?

BIRDBOOT: What?

MOON: You think he's Magnus in disguise?

BIRDBOOT: I don't think you're concentrating, Moon.

MOON: I thought you said—

BIRDBOOT: You keep chattering on about Higgs and Puckeridge—what's the matter with you?

MOON (*thoughtfully*): I wonder if they talk about me . . . ?

A strange impulse makes SIMON *turn on the radio.*

RADIO: Here is another police message. Essex County police are still searching in vain for the madman who is at large in the deadly marshes of the coastal region. Inspector Hound who is masterminding the operation, is not available for comment but it is widely believed that he has a secret plan. . . . Meanwhile police and volunteers are combing the swamps with loud-hailers, shouting, "Don't be a

19

madman, give yourself up." That is the end of the police message.

SIMON *turns off the radio. He is clearly nervous.* MOON *and* BIRDBOOT *are on separate tracks.*

BIRDBOOT (*knowingly*): Oh yes . . .

MOON: Yes, I should think my name is seldom off Puckeridge's lips . . . sad, really. I mean, it's no life at all, a stand-in's stand-in.

BIRDBOOT: Yes . . . yes . . .

MOON: Higgs never gives me a second thought. I can tell by the way he nods.

BIRDBOOT: Revenge, of course.

MOON: What?

BIRDBOOT: Jealousy.

MOON: Nonsense—there's nothing *personal* in it—

BIRDBOOT: The paranoid grudge—

MOON (*sharply first, then starting to career* . . .): It is merely that it is not enough to wax at another's wane, to be held in reserve, to be on hand, on call, to step in or not at all, the substitute—the near offer —the temporary-acting—for I am Moon, continuous Moon, in my own shoes, Moon in June, April, September and no member of the human race keeps warm my bit of space—yes, I can tell by the way he nods.

BIRDBOOT: Quite mad, of course.

MOON: What?

BIRDBOOT: The answer lies out there in the swamps.

MOON: Oh.

BIRDBOOT: The skeleton in the cupboard is coming home to roost.

MOON: Oh yes. (*He clears his throat . . . for both he and*

20

BIRDBOOT *have a "public" voice, a critic voice which they turn on for sustained pronouncements of opinion.*) Already in the opening stages we note the classic impact of the catalystic figure—the outsider —plunging through to the centre of an ordered world and setting up the disruptions—the shock waves—which unless I am much mistaken, will strip these comfortable people—these crustaceans in the rock pool of society—strip them of their shells and leave them exposed as the trembling raw meat which, at heart, is all of us. But there is more to it than that—

BIRDBOOT: I agree—keep your eye on Magnus.

A tennis ball bounces through the French windows, closely followed by FELICITY, *who is in her twenties. She wears a pretty tennis outfit, and carries a racket.*

FELICITY (*calling behind her*): Out!

It takes her a moment to notice SIMON *who is standing shiftily to one side.* MOON *is stirred by a memory.*

MOON: I say, Birdboot . . .
BIRDBOOT: That's the one.
FELICITY (*catching sight of* SIMON): You!

Felicity's manner at the moment is one of great surprise but some pleasure.

SIMON (*nervously*): Er, yes—hello again.
FELICITY: What are you doing here?
SIMON: Well, I . . .

21

MOON: She's—

BIRDBOOT: Sssh . . .

SIMON: No doubt you're surprised to see me.

FELICITY: Honestly, darling, you really are extraordinary.

SIMON: Yes, well, here I am.

FELICITY: You must have been desperate to see me—I mean, I'm *flattered*, but couldn't it wait till I got back?

SIMON (*bravely*): There is something you don't know.

FELICITY: What is it?

SIMON: Look, about the things I said—it may be that I got carried away a little—we both did—

FELICITY (*stiffly*): What are you trying to say?

SIMON: I love another!

FELICITY: I see.

SIMON: I didn't make any promises—I merely—

FELICITY: You don't have to say any more—

SIMON: Oh, I didn't want to hurt you—

FELICITY: Of all the nerve!

SIMON: Well, I—

FELICITY: You philandering coward—

SIMON: Let me explain—

FELICITY: This is hardly the time and place—you think you can barge in anywhere, whatever I happen to be doing—

SIMON: But I want you to know that my admiration for you is sincere—I don't want you to think that I didn't mean those things I said—

FELICITY: I'll kill you for this, Simon Gascoyne!

She leaves in tears, passing MRS. DRUDGE *who has entered in time to overhear her last remark.*

22

MOON: It was her.

BIRDBOOT: I told you—straight to the top—

MOON: No, no—

BIRDBOOT: Sssh. . . .

SIMON (*to* MRS. DRUDGE): Yes, what is it?

MRS. DRUDGE: I have come to set up the card table, sir.

SIMON: I don't think I can stay.

MRS. DRUDGE: Oh, Lady Muldoon *will* be disappointed.

SIMON: Does she know I'm here?

MRS. DRUDGE: Oh yes, sir, I just told her and it put her in quite a tizzy.

SIMON: Really? . . . Well, I suppose now that I've cleared the air . . . Quite a tizzy, you say . . . really . . . really . . .

He and MRS. DRUDGE *start setting up for card game.* MRS. DRUDGE *leaves when this is done.*

MOON: Felicity!—she's the one.

BIRDBOOT: Nonsense—red herring.

MOON: I mean, it was *her!*

BIRDBOOT (*exasperated*): *What* was?

MOON: That lady I saw you with last night!

BIRDBOOT (*inhales with fury*): Are you suggesting that a man of my scrupulous integrity would trade his pen for a mess of pottage?! Simply because in the course of my profession I happen to have struck up an acquaintance—to have, that is, a warm regard, if you like, for a fellow toiler in the vineyard of greasepaint—I find it simply intolerable to be pillified and viloried—

MOON: I never implied—

BIRDBOOT: —to find myself the object of uninformed malice, the petty slanders of little men—

23

MOON: I'm sorry—

BIRDBOOT: —to suggest that my good opinion in a journal of unimpeachable integrity is at the disposal of the first coquette who gives me what I want—

MOON: Sssssh—

BIRDBOOT: A ladies' man! . . . Why, Myrtle and I have been together now for—Christ!—who's *that?*

Enter LADY CYNTHIA MULDOON *through French windows. A beautiful woman in her thirties. She wears a cocktail dress, is formally coiffured, and carries a tennis racket.*

Her effect on BIRDBOOT *is also impressive. He half-rises and sinks back agape.*

CYNTHIA (*entering*): Simon!

A dramatic freeze between her and SIMON.

MOON: Lady Muldoon.

BIRDBOOT: No, I mean—who *is* she?

SIMON (*coming forward*): Cynthia!

CYNTHIA: Don't say anything for a moment—just hold me.

He seizes her and glues his lips to hers, as they say. While their lips are glued—

BIRDBOOT: She's *beautiful*—a vision of eternal grace, a poem . . .

MOON: I think she's got her mouth open.

CYNTHIA *breaks away dramatically.*

CYNTHIA: We can't go on meeting like this!

SIMON: We have nothing to be ashamed of!

CYNTHIA: But darling, this is madness!

SIMON: Yes!—I am mad with love for you!

CYNTHIA: Please—remember where we are!

SIMON: Cynthia, I love you!

CYNTHIA: Don't—I love Albert!

SIMON: He's dead! (*Shaking her.*) Do you understand me—Albert's dead!

CYNTHIA: No—I'll never give up hope! Let me go! We are not free!

SIMON: I don't care, we were meant for each other— had we but met in time.

CYNTHIA: You're a cad, Simon! You will use me and cast me aside as you have cast aside so many others.

SIMON: No, Cynthia!—you can make me a better person!

CYNTHIA: You're ruthless—so strong, so cruel—

Ruthlessly he kisses her.

MOON: The son she never had, now projected in this handsome stranger and transformed into lover— youth, vigour, the animal, the athlete as aesthete —breaking down the barriers at the deepest level of desire.

BIRDBOOT: By jove, I think you're right. Her mouth *is* open.

CYNTHIA *breaks away.* MRS. DRUDGE *has entered.*

CYNTHIA: Stop—can't you see you're making a fool of yourself!

SIMON: I'll kill anyone who comes between us!

CYNTHIA: Yes, what is it, Mrs. Drudge?

MRS. DRUDGE: Should I close the windows, my lady? The fog is beginning to roll off the sea like a deadly—

CYNTHIA: Yes, you'd better. It looks as if we're in for one of those days. Are the cards ready?

MRS. DRUDGE: Yes, my lady.

CYNTHIA: Would you tell Miss Cunningham we are waiting.

MRS. DRUDGE: Yes, my lady.

CYNTHIA: And fetch the Major down.

MRS. DRUDGE (*as she leaves*): I think I hear him coming downstairs now.

She does: the sound of a wheelchair approaching down several flights of stairs with landings in between. It arrives bearing MAGNUS *at about 15 m.p.h., knocking* SIMON *over violently.*

CYNTHIA: Simon!

MAGNUS (*roaring*): Never had a chance! Ran under the wheels!

CYNTHIA: Darling, are you all right?

MAGNUS: I have witnesses!

CYNTHIA: Oh, Simon—say something!

SIMON (*sitting up suddenly*): I'm most frightfully sorry.

MAGNUS (*still shouting*): How long have you been a pedestrian?

SIMON: Ever since I could walk.

CYNTHIA: Can you walk now . . . ?

SIMON *rises and walks.*

Thank God! Magnus, this is Simon Gascoyne.

MAGNUS: What's he doing here?

CYNTHIA: He just turned up.

MAGNUS: Really? How do you like it here?

SIMON (*to* CYNTHIA): I could stay forever.

FELICITY *enters.*

FELICITY: So— You're still here.

CYNTHIA: Of course he's still here. We're going to play cards. There's no need to introduce you two, is there, for I recall now that you, Simon, met me through Felicity, our mutual friend.

FELICITY: Yes, Simon is an old friend, though not as old as you, Cynthia dear.

SIMON: Yes, I haven't seen Felicity since—

FELICITY: Last night.

CYNTHIA: Indeed? Well, you deal, Felicity. Simon, you help me with the sofa. Will you partner Felicity, Magnus, against Simon and me?

MAGNUS (*aside*): Will Simon and you always be partnered against me, Cynthia?

CYNTHIA: What do you mean, Magnus?

MAGNUS: You are a damned attractive woman, Cynthia.

CYNTHIA: Please! Please! Remember Albert!

MAGNUS: Albert's dead, Cynthia—and you are still young. I'm sure he would have wished that you and I—

CYNTHIA: No, Magnus, this is not to be!

MAGNUS: It's Gascoyne, isn't it? I'll kill him if he comes between us.

CYNTHIA (*calling*): Simon!

The sofa is shoved towards the card table, once more revealing the corpse, though not to the players.

BIRDBOOT: Simon's for the chop all right.

CYNTHIA: Right! Who starts?

MAGNUS: I do. No bid.

They start playing, putting down and picking up cards.

27

CYNTHIA: Did I hear you say you saw Felicity last night, Simon?

SIMON: Did I?—Ah yes, yes quite—your turn, Felicity.

FELICITY: I've had my turn, haven't I, Simon?—now, it seems, it's Cynthia's turn.

CYNTHIA: That's my trick, Felicity dear.

FELICITY: Hell hath no fury like a woman scorned, Simon.

SIMON: Yes, I've heard it said.

FELICITY: So I hope you have not been cheating, Simon.

SIMON (*standing up and throwing down his cards*): No, Felicity, it's just that I hold the cards!

CYNTHIA: Well done, Simon!

MAGNUS *pays* SIMON *generously in blank notes, while* CYNTHIA *deals.*

FELICITY: Strange how Simon appeared in the neighbourhood from nowhere. We know so little about him.

SIMON: It doesn't always pay to show your hand!

CYNTHIA: Right! Simon, it's your opening on the minor bid.

SIMON *plays.*

CYNTHIA: Hm, let's see. . . . (*Plays.*)

FELICITY: I hear there's a dangerous madman on the loose.

CYNTHIA: Simon?

SIMON: Yes—yes—sorry. (*Plays.*)

CYNTHIA: I meld.

FELICITY: Yes—personally, I think he's been hiding out in the deserted cottage on the cliffs (*plays*).

SIMON: Flush!

CYNTHIA: No! Simon—your luck's in tonight!

28

FELICITY: We shall see—the night is not over yet, Simon Gascoyne! (*She exits.*)

Once more MAGNUS *pays* SIMON.

SIMON (*to* MAGNUS): So you're the crippled half-brother of Lord Muldoon who turned up out of the blue from Canada just the other day, are you? It's taken you a long time to get here. What did you do—walk? Oh, I say, I'm most frightfully sorry!

MAGNUS: Care for a spin round the rose garden, Cynthia?

CYNTHIA: No Magnus, I must talk to Simon.

SIMON: My round, I think, Major.

MAGNUS: You think so?

SIMON: Yes, Major—I do.

MAGNUS: There's an old Canadian proverb handed down from the Blackfoot Indians, which says: He who laughs last laughs longest.

SIMON: Yes, I've heard it said.

CYNTHIA (*calling*): Simon!

MAGNUS: Well, I think I'll go and oil my gun. (*He exits.*)

CYNTHIA: I think Magnus suspects something. And Felicity . . . Simon, was there anything between you and Felicity?

SIMON: No, no—it's over between her and me, Cynthia—it was a mere passing fleeting thing we had—but now that I have found you—

CYNTHIA: If I find that you have been untrue to me—if I find that you have falsely seduced me from my dear husband Albert—I will kill you, Simon Gascoyne!

MRS. DRUDGE *has entered silently to witness this. On this tableau, pregnant with significance, the*

29

act ends, the body still undiscovered. Perfunctory applause.

MOON *and* BIRDBOOT *seem to be completely preoccupied, becoming audible, as it were.*

MOON: Camps it around the Old Vic in his opera cloak and passes me the tat.

BIRDBOOT: Do you believe in love at first sight?

MOON: It's not that I think I'm a better critic—

BIRDBOOT: I feel my whole life changing—

MOON: I am but it's not that.

BIRDBOOT: Oh, the world will laugh at me, I know . . .

MOON: It is not that they are much in the way of shoes to step into . . .

BIRDBOOT: . . . call me an infatuated old fool . . .

MOON: . . . They are not.

BIRDBOOT: . . . condemn me . . .

MOON: He is standing in my light, that is all.

BIRDBOOT: . . . betrayer of my class . . .

MOON: . . . an almost continuous eclipse, interrupted by the phenomenon of moonlight.

BIRDBOOT: I don't care, I'm a goner.

MOON: And I dream . . .

BIRDBOOT: The Blue Angel all over again.

MOON: . . . of the day his temperature climbs through the top of his head . . .

BIRDBOOT: Ah, the sweet madness of love . . .

MOON: . . . of the spasm on the stairs . . .

BIRDBOOT: Myrtle, farewell . . .

MOON: . . . dreaming of the stair he'll never reach—

BIRDBOOT: —for I only live but once. . . .

MOON: Sometimes I dream that I've killed him.

BIRDBOOT: What?

MOON: What?

They pull themselves together.

BIRDBOOT: Yes . . . yes. . . . A beautiful performance, a collector's piece. I shall say so.

MOON: A very promising debut. I'll put in a good word.

BIRDBOOT: It would be as hypocritical of me to withhold praise on grounds of personal feelings, as to withhold censure.

MOON: You're right. Courageous.

BIRDBOOT: Oh, I know what people will say— There goes Birdboot buttering up his latest—

MOON: Ignore them—

BIRDBOOT: But I rise above that— The fact is I genuinely believe her performance to be one of the summits in the range of contemporary theatre.

MOON: Trim-buttocked, that's the word for her.

BIRDBOOT: —the radiance, the inner sadness—

MOON: Does she actually come across with it?

BIRDBOOT: The part as written is a mere cypher but she manages to make Cynthia a real person—

MOON: *Cynthia?*

BIRDBOOT: And should she, as a result, care to meet me over a drink, simply by way of er—thanking me, as it were—

MOON: Well, you fickle old bastard!

BIRDBOOT (*aggressively*): Are you suggesting . . . ? (*He shudders to a halt and clears his throat.*) Well now—shaping up quite nicely, wouldn't you say?

MOON: Oh yes, yes. A nice trichotomy of forces. One must reserve judgement of course, until the confrontation, but I think it's pretty clear where we're heading.

31

BIRDBOOT: I agree. It's Magnus a mile off.

Small pause.

MOON: What's Magnus a mile off?

BIRDBOOT: If we knew that we wouldn't be here.

MOON (*clears throat*): Let me at once say that it has *élan* while at the same time avoiding *éclat*. Having said that, and I think it must be said, I am bound to ask—does this play know where it is going?

BIRDBOOT: Well, it seems open and shut to me, Moon— Magnus is not what he pretends to be and he's got his next victim marked down—

MOON: Does it, I repeat, declare its affiliations? There are moments, and I would not begrudge it this, when the play, if we can call it that, and I think on balance we can, aligns itself uncompromisingly on the side of life. *Je suis*, it seems to be saying, *ergo sum*. But is that enough? I think we are entitled to ask. For what in fact is this play concerned with? It is my belief that here we are concerned with what I have referred to elsewhere as the nature of identity. I think we are entitled to ask—and here one is irresistibly reminded of Voltaire's cry, *"Voilà"*—I think we are entitled to ask— *Where is God?*

BIRDBOOT (*stunned*): Who?

MOON: Go-od.

BIRDBOOT (*peeping furtively into his programme*): God?

MOON: I think we are entitled to ask.

The phone rings.

The set re-illumines to reveal CYNTHIA, FELICITY *and* MAGNUS *about to take coffee, which is being*

32

taken round by MRS. DRUDGE. SIMON *is missing. The body lies in position.*

MRS. DRUDGE (*into phone*): The same, half an hour later? . . . No, I'm sorry—there's no one of that name here. (*She replaces phone and goes round with coffee. To* CYNTHIA.) Black or white, my lady?
CYNTHIA: White please.

> MRS. DRUDGE *pours.*

MRS. DRUDGE (*to* FELICITY): Black or white, miss?
FELICITY: White please.

> MRS. DRUDGE *pours.*

MRS. DRUDGE (*to* MAGNUS): Black or white, Major?
MAGNUS: White please.

> *Ditto.*

MRS. DRUDGE (*to* CYNTHIA): Sugar, my lady?
CYNTHIA: Yes please.

> *Puts sugar in.*

MRS. DRUDGE (*to* FELICITY): Sugar, miss?
FELICITY: Yes please.

> *Ditto.*

MRS. DRUDGE (*to* MAGNUS): Sugar, Major?
MAGNUS: Yes please.

> *Ditto.*

> MRS. DRUDGE *leaves, and reappears with a plate of biscuits.*

MRS. DRUDGE (*to* CYNTHIA): Biscuit, my lady?
CYNTHIA: No thank you.

BIRDBOOT (*writing elaborately in his notebook*): The second act, however, fails to fulfill the promise . . .

FELICITY: If you ask me, there's something funny going on.

Mrs. Drudge's approach to FELICITY *makes* FELICITY *jump to her feet in impatience. She goes to the radio while* MAGNUS *declines his biscuit, and* MRS. DRUDGE *leaves.*

RADIO: We interrupt our programme for a special police message. The search for the dangerous madman who is on the loose in Essex has now narrowed to the immediate vicinity of Muldoon Manor. Police are hampered by the deadly swamps and the fog, but believe that the madman spent last night in a deserted cottage on the cliffs. The public is advised to stick together and make sure none of their number is missing. That is the end of the police message.

FELICITY *turns off the radio nervously. Pause.*

CYNTHIA: Where's Simon?

FELICITY: Who?

CYNTHIA: Simon. Have you seen him?

FELICITY: No.

CYNTHIA: Have you, Magnus?

MAGNUS: No.

CYNTHIA: Oh.

FELICITY: Yes, there's something foreboding in the air, it is as if one of *us*—

CYNTHIA: Oh, Felicity, the house is locked up tight—no one can get in—and the police are practically on the doorstep.

FELICITY: I don't know—it's just a feeling.

34

CYNTHIA: It's only the fog.

MAGNUS: Hound will never get through on a day like this—

CYNTHIA (*shouting at him*): *Fog!*

FELICITY: He means the Inspector.

CYNTHIA: Is he bringing a dog?

FELICITY: Not that I know of.

MAGNUS: —never get through the swamps. Yes, I'm afraid the madman can show his hand in safety now.

A mournful baying, hooting is heard in the distance, scary.

CYNTHIA: What's that?!

FELICITY (*tensely*): It sounded like the cry of a gigantic hound!

BIRDBOOT: Rings a bell.

MAGNUS: Poor devil!

CYNTHIA: Ssssh!

They listen. The sound is repeated, nearer.

FELICITY: There it is again!

CYNTHIA: It's coming this way—it's right outside the house!

MRS. DRUDGE *enters.*

MRS. DRUDGE: Inspector Hound!

CYNTHIA: A *police* dog?

Enter INSPECTOR HOUND. *On his feet are his swamp boots. These are two inflatable—and inflated—pontoons with flat bottoms about two feet across. He carries a foghorn.*

HOUND: Lady Muldoon?

35

CYNTHIA: Yes.

HOUND: I came as soon as I could. Where shall I put my foghorn and my swamp boots?

CYNTHIA: Mrs. Drudge will take them out. Be prepared, as the Force's motto has it, eh, Inspector? How very resourceful!

HOUND (*divesting himself of boots and foghorn*): It takes more than a bit of weather to keep a policeman from his duty.

MRS. DRUDGE *leaves with chattels. A pause.*

CYNTHIA: Oh—er, Inspector Hound—Felicity Cunningham, Major Magnus Muldoon.

HOUND: Good evening.

He and CYNTHIA *continue to look expectantly at each other.*

CYNTHIA *and* HOUND (*together*): Well?—Sorry—

CYNTHIA: No, do go on.

HOUND: Thank you. Well, tell me about it in your own words—take your time, begin at the beginning and don't leave anything out.

CYNTHIA: I beg your pardon?

HOUND: Fear nothing. You are in safe hands now. I hope you haven't touched anything.

CYNTHIA: I'm afraid I don't understand.

HOUND: I'm Inspector Hound.

CYNTHIA: Yes.

HOUND: Well, what's it all about?

CYNTHIA: I really have no idea.

HOUND: How did it begin?

CYNTHIA: What?

HOUND: The . . . thing.

36

CYNTHIA: What thing?

HOUND (*rapidly losing confidence but exasperated*): The trouble!

CYNTHIA: There hasn't *been* any trouble!

HOUND: Didn't you phone the police?

CYNTHIA: No.

FELICITY: I didn't.

MAGNUS: What for?

HOUND: I see. (*Pause.*) This puts me in a very difficult position. (*A steady pause.*) Well, I'll be getting along, then. (*He moves towards the door.*)

CYNTHIA: I'm terribly sorry.

HOUND (*stiffly*): That's perfectly all right.

CYNTHIA: Thank you so much for coming.

HOUND: Not at all. You never know, there might have been a serious matter.

CYNTHIA: Drink?

HOUND: More serious than that, even.

CYNTHIA (*correcting*): Drink before you go?

HOUND: No thank you. (*Leaves.*)

CYNTHIA (*through the door*): I do hope you find him.

HOUND (*reappearing at once*): Find who, Madam?— out with it!

CYNTHIA: I thought you were looking for the lunatic.

HOUND: And what do you know about that?

CYNTHIA: It was on the radio.

HOUND: Was it, indeed? Well, that's what I'm here about, really. I didn't want to mention it because I didn't know how much you knew. No point in causing unnecessary panic, even with a murderer in our midst.

FELICITY: Murderer, did you say?

HOUND: Ah—so that was not on the radio?

CYNTHIA: Whom has he murdered, Inspector?

HOUND: Perhaps no one—yet. Let us hope we are in time.

MAGNUS: You believe he is in our midst, Inspector?

HOUND: I do. If anyone of you have recently encountered a youngish good-looking fellow in a smart suit, white shirt, hatless, well-spoken—someone possibly claiming to have just moved into the neighbourhood, someone who on the surface seems as sane as you or I, then now is the time to speak!

FELICITY: . . . I . . .

HOUND: Don't interrupt!

FELICITY: Inspector . . .

HOUND: Very well.

CYNTHIA: No. Felicity!

HOUND: Please, Lady Cynthia, we are all in this together. I must ask you to put yourself completely in my hands.

CYNTHIA: Don't, Inspector. I love Albert.

HOUND: I don't think you quite grasp my meaning.

MAGNUS: Is one of us in danger, Inspector?

HOUND: Didn't it strike you as odd that on his escape the madman made a beeline for Muldoon Manor? It is my guess that he bears a deep-seated grudge against someone in this very house! Lady Muldoon—where is your husband?

CYNTHIA: My husband?—you don't mean—?

HOUND: I don't know—but I have a reason to believe that one of you is the real McCoy!

FELICITY: The real what?

HOUND: William Herbert McCoy who as a young man, meeting the madman in the street and being solicited for sixpence for a cup of tea, replied,

"Why don't you do a decent day's work, you shifty old bag of horse manure," in Canada all those many years ago and went on to make his fortune. (*He starts to pace intensely.*) The madman was a mere boy at the time but he never forgot that moment, and thenceforth carried in his heart the promise of revenge! (*At which point he finds himself standing on top of the corpse. He looks down carefully.*) Is there anything you have forgotten to tell me?

They all see the corpse for the first time.

FELICITY: So the madman has struck!

CYNTHIA: Oh—it's horrible—horrible—

HOUND: Yes, just as I feared. Now you see the sort of man you are protecting.

CYNTHIA: I can't believe it!

FELICITY: I'll have to tell him, Cynthia—Inspector, a stranger of that description has indeed appeared in our midst—Simon Gascoyne. Oh, he had charm, I'll give you that, and he took me in completely. I'm afraid I made a fool of myself over him, and so did Cynthia.

HOUND: Where is he now?

MAGNUS: He must be around the house—he couldn't get away in these conditions.

HOUND: You're right. Fear naught, Lady Muldoon—I shall apprehend the man who killed your husband.

CYNTHIA: My husband? I don't understand.

HOUND: Everything points to Gascoyne.

CYNTHIA: But who's that? (*The corpse.*)

HOUND: Your husband.

CYNTHIA: No, it's not.

HOUND: Yes, it is.

CYNTHIA: I tell you it's not.

HOUND: Are you sure?

CYNTHIA: For goodness sake!

HOUND: Then who is it?

CYNTHIA: I don't know.

HOUND: Anybody?

FELICITY: I've never seen him before.

MAGNUS: Quite unlike anybody I've ever met.

HOUND: I seem to have made a dreadful mistake. Lady Muldoon, I do apologize.

CYNTHIA: But what are we going to do?

HOUND (*snatching the phone*): I'll phone the police!

CYNTHIA: But you are the police!

HOUND: Thank God I'm here—the lines have been cut!

CYNTHIA: You mean—?

HOUND: Yes!—we're on our own, cut off from the world and in grave danger!

FELICITY: You mean—?

HOUND: Yes!—I think the killer will strike again!

MAGNUS: You mean—?

HOUND: Yes! One of us ordinary mortals thrown together by fate and cut off by the elements, is the murderer! He must be found—search the house!

All depart speedily in different directions leaving a momentarily empty stage. SIMON *strolls on.*

SIMON (*entering, calling*): Anyone about?—funny . . . (*He notices the corpse and is surprised. He approaches it and turns it over. He stands up and looks about in alarm.*)

BIRDBOOT: This is where Simon gets the chap.

There is a shot. SIMON *falls dead.*

40

INSPECTOR HOUND *runs on and crouches down by Simon's body.* CYNTHIA *appears at the French windows. She stops there and stares.*

CYNTHIA: What happened, Inspector?!

HOUND *turns to face her.*

HOUND: He's dead . . . Simon Gascoyne, I presume. Rough justice even for a killer—unless—unless—We assumed that the body could not have been lying there before Simon Gascoyne entered the house . . . but . . . (*he slides the sofa over the body*) . . . there's your answer. And now—who killed Simon Gascoyne? And why?

"Curtain," Freeze, Applause, Exeunt.

MOON: Why not?

BIRDBOOT: Exactly. Good riddance.

MOON: Yes, getting away with murder must be quite easy provided that one's motive is sufficiently inscrutable.

BIRDBOOT: Fickle young pup! He was deceiving her right, left and centre.

MOON (*thoughtfully*): Of course, I'd still have Puckeridge behind *me* . . .

BIRDBOOT: She needs someone steadier, more mature . . .

MOON: . . . And if I could, so could he . . .

BIRDBOOT: Yes, I know of this rather nice hotel, very discreet, run by a man of the world. . . .

MOON: Uneasy lies the head that wears the crown.

BIRDBOOT: Breakfast served in one's room and no questions asked.

MOON: Does Puckeridge dream of me?

BIRDBOOT (*pause*): Hello—what's happened?

MOON: What? Oh yes—what do you make of it, so far?

BIRDBOOT (*clears throat*): It is at this point that the play, for me, comes alive. The groundwork has been well and truly laid, and the author has taken the trouble to learn from the masters of the genre. He has created a real situation, and few will doubt his ability to resolve it with a startling dénouement. Certainly that is what it so far lacks, but it has a beginning, a middle and I have no doubt it will prove to have an end. For this let us give thanks, and double thanks for a good clean show without a trace of smut. But perhaps even all this would be for nothing were it not for a performance which I consider to be one of the summits in the range of contemporary theatre. In what is possibly the finest Cynthia since the war—

MOON: If we examine this more closely, and I think close examination is the least tribute that this play deserves, I think we will find that within the austere framework of what is seen to be on one level a country-house week-end, and what a useful symbol that is, the author has given us—yes, I will go so far—he has given us the human condition—

BIRDBOOT: More talent in her little finger—

MOON: An uncanny ear that might have belonged to a Van Gogh—

BIRDBOOT: —a public scandal that the Birthday Honours to date have neglected—

MOON: Faced as we are with such ubiquitous obliquity, it is hard, it is hard indeed, and therefore I will not attempt, to refrain from invoking the names of Kafka, Sartre, Shakespeare, St. Paul, Beckett, Birkett, Pinero, Pirandello, Dante and Dorothy L. Sayers.

BIRDBOOT: A rattling good evening out. I was held.

The phone starts to ring on the empty stage. MOON *tries to ignore it.*

MOON: Harder still— Harder still if possible— Harder still if it is possible to be— Neither do I find it easy— Dante and Dorothy L. Sayers. Harder still—
BIRDBOOT: Others taking part included—*Moon!*

For MOON *has lost patience and is bearing down on the ringing phone. He is frankly irritated.*

MOON (*picking up phone, barks*): Hel-lo! (*Pause, turns to* BIRDBOOT, *quietly.*) It's for you.

Pause.

BIRDBOOT *gets up. He approaches cautiously.* MOON *gives him the phone and moves back to his seat.* BIRDBOOT *watches him go. He looks round and smiles weakly, expiating himself.*

BIRDBOOT (*into phone*): Hello. . . . (*Explosion.*) Oh, for God's sake, Myrtle—I've told you never to phone me at work! (*He is naturally embarrassed, looking about with surreptitious fury.*) What? Last night? Good God, woman, this is hardly the time to—I assure you, Myrtle, there is absolutely nothing going on between me and—. I took her to dinner simply by way of keeping *au fait* with the world of the paint and the motley—yes, I promise—Yes, I do—Yes, I *said* yes—I *do*—and you are mine too, Myrtle—darling—I can't—(*whispers*) *I'm not alone* —(*Up.*) No, she's not!—(*He looks around furtively, licks his lips and mumbles.*) All *right!* I love your

43

little pink ears and you are my own fluffy bunny-boo— Now for God's sake— Good-bye, Myrtle— (*puts down phone*).

BIRDBOOT *mops his brow with his handkerchief. As he turns, a tennis ball bounces in through the French windows, followed by* FELICITY, *as before, in tennis outfit. The lighting is as it was. Everything is as it was. It is, let us say, the same moment of time.*

FELICITY (*calling*): Out! (*She catches sight of* BIRDBOOT *and is amazed.*) You!

BIRDBOOT: Er, yes—hello again.

FELICITY: What are you doing here?!

BIRDBOOT: Well, I . . .

FELICITY: Honestly, darling, you really are extraordinary—

BIRDBOOT: Yes, well, here I am. (*He looks round sheepishly.*)

FELICITY: You must have been desperate to see me—I mean, I'm flattered, but couldn't it wait till I got back?

BIRDBOOT: No, no, you've got it all wrong—

FELICITY: What is it?

BIRDBOOT: And about last night—perhaps I gave you the wrong impression—got carried away a bit, perhaps—

FELICITY (*stiffly*): What are you trying to say?

BIRDBOOT: I want to call it off.

FELICITY: I see.

BIRDBOOT: I didn't promise anything—and the fact is, I have my reputation—people do talk—

FELICITY: You don't have to say any more—

44

BIRDBOOT: And my wife, too—I don't know how she got to hear of it, but—

FELICITY: Of all the nerve!

BIRDBOOT: I'm sorry you had to find out like this—the fact is I didn't mean it this way—

FELICITY: You philandering coward!

BIRDBOOT: I'm sorry—but I want you to know that I meant those things I said—oh yes—shows brilliant promise—I shall say so—

FELICITY: I'll kill you for this, Simon Gascoyne!

She leaves in tears, passing MRS. DRUDGE *who has entered in time to overhear her last remark.*

BIRDBOOT (*wide-eyed*): Good God . . .

MRS. DRUDGE: I have come to set up the card table, sir.

BIRDBOOT (*wildly*): I can't stay for a game of *cards!*

MRS. DRUDGE: Oh, Lady Muldoon *will* be disappointed.

BIRDBOOT: You mean . . . you mean, she wants to meet me . . . ?

MRS. DRUDGE: Oh yes, sir, I just told her and it put her in quite a tizzy.

BIRDBOOT: Really? Yes, well, a man of my influence is not to be sneezed at—I think I have some small name for the making of reputations—mmm, yes, quite a tizzy, you say?

MRS. DRUDGE *is busied with the card table.* BIRDBOOT *stands marooned and bemused for a moment.*

MOON (*from his seat*): Birdboot!—(*a tense whisper*)—Birdboot!

BIRDBOOT *looks round vaguely.*

What the hell are you doing?

BIRDBOOT: Nothing.

MOON: Stop making an ass of yourself. Come back.

BIRDBOOT: Oh, I know what you're thinking—but the fact is I genuinely consider her performance to be one of the summits—

CYNTHIA *enters as before.* MRS. DRUDGE *has gone.*

CYNTHIA: Darling!

BIRDBOOT: Ah, good evening—may I say that I genuinely consider—

CYNTHIA: Don't say anything for a moment—just hold me. (*She falls into his arms.*)

BIRDBOOT: All right!—let us throw off the hollow pretences of the gimcrack codes we live by! Dear lady, from the first moment I saw you, I felt my whole life changing—

CYNTHIA (*breaking free*): We can't go on meeting like this!

BIRDBOOT: I am not ashamed to proclaim nightly my love for you!—but fortunately that will not be necessary—I know of a very good hotel, discreet—run by a man of the world—

CYNTHIA: But darling, this is madness!

BIRDBOOT: Yes! I am mad with love.

CYNTHIA: Please!—remember where we are!

BIRDBOOT: I don't care! Let them think what they like, I love you!

CYNTHIA: Don't—I love Albert!

BIRDBOOT: He's dead. (*Shaking her.*) Do you understand me—Albert's dead!

CYNTHIA: No—I'll never give up hope! Let me go! We are not free!

BIRDBOOT: You mean Myrtle? She means nothing to me—

46

nothing!—she's all cocoa and blue nylon fur slip-pers—not a spark of creative genius in her whole slumping knee-length-knickered body—

CYNTHIA: You're a cad, Simon! You will use me and cast me aside as you have cast aside so many others!

BIRDBOOT: No, Cynthia—now that I have found you—

CYNTHIA: You're ruthless—so strong—so cruel—

BIRDBOOT *seizes her in an embrace, during which* MRS. DRUDGE *enters, and Moon's fevered voice is heard.*

MOON: Have you taken leave of your tiny mind?

CYNTHIA *breaks free.*

CYNTHIA: Stop—can't you see you're making a fool of yourself!

MOON: She's right.

BIRDBOOT (*to* MOON): You keep out of this.

CYNTHIA: Yes, what is it, Mrs. Drudge?

MRS. DRUDGE: Should I close the windows, my lady? The fog—

CYNTHIA: Yes, you'd better.

MOON: Look, they've got your number—

BIRDBOOT: I'll leave in my own time, thank you very much.

MOON: It's the finish of you, I suppose you know that—

BIRDBOOT: I don't need your twopenny Grubb Street prognostications—I have found something bigger and finer—

MOON (*bemused, to himself*): If only it were Higgs. . .

CYNTHIA: . . . And fetch the Major down.

MRS. DRUDGE: I think I hear him coming downstairs now.

47

She leaves. The sound of a wheelchair's approach as before. BIRDBOOT *prudently keeps out of the chair's former path but it enters from the next wing down and knocks him flying. A babble of anguish and protestation.*

CYNTHIA: Simon—say something!
BIRDBOOT: That reckless bastard (*as he sits up*).
CYNTHIA: Thank God!—
MAGNUS: What's *he* doing here?
CYNTHIA: He just turned up.
MAGNUS: Really? How do you like it here?
BIRDBOOT: I couldn't take it night after night.
    FELICITY *enters.*
FELICITY: So—you're still here.
CYNTHIA: Of course he's still here. We're going to play cards. There is no need to introduce you two, is there, for I recall now that you, Simon, met me through Felicity, our mutual friend.
FELICITY: Yes, Simon is an old friend . . .
BIRDBOOT: Ah—yes—well I like to give young up-and-comers the benefit of my—er—of course, she lacks technique as yet—
FELICITY: Last night.
BIRDBOOT: I'm not talking about last night!
CYNTHIA: Indeed? Well, you deal, Felicity. Simon, you help me with the sofa.

    CYNTHIA *and* MAGNUS *confer as in the earlier scene.*

BIRDBOOT (*to* MOON): Did you see that? Tried to kill me. I told you it was Magnus—not that it *is* Magnus.
MOON: Who did it, you mean?
BIRDBOOT: What?
MOON: You think it's not Magnus who did it?

48

BIRDBOOT: Get a grip on yourself, Moon—the facts are staring you in the face. He's after Cynthia for one thing.

MAGNUS: It's Gascoyne, isn't it?

BIRDBOOT: Over my dead body!

MAGNUS: If he comes between us . . .

MOON (*angrily*): For God's sake sit down!

CYNTHIA: Simon!

BIRDBOOT: She needs me, Moon. I've got to make up a four.

CYNTHIA *and* BIRDBOOT *move the sofa as before, and they all sit at the table.*

CYNTHIA: Right! Who starts?

MAGNUS: I do. I'll dummy for a no-bid ruff and double my holding on South's queen (*while he moves cards*).

CYNTHIA: Did I hear you say you saw Felicity last night, Simon?

BIRDBOOT: Er—er—

FELICITY: Pay twenty-ones or trump my contract. (*Discards.*) Cynthia's turn.

CYNTHIA: I'll trump your contract with five dummy no-trumps there (*discards*), and I'll move West's rook for the re-bid with a banker ruff on his second trick there. (*Discards.*) Simon?

BIRDBOOT: Would you mind doing that again?

CYNTHIA: And I'll ruff your dummy with five no-bid trumps there (*discards*), and I support your re-bid with a banker for the solo ruff in the dummy trick there. (*Discards.*)

BIRDBOOT (*standing up and throwing down his cards*): And I call your bluff!

CYNTHIA: Well done, Simon!

MAGNUS *pays* BIRDBOOT *while* CYNTHIA *deals.*

FELICITY: Strange how Simon appeared in the neighbourhood from nowhere, we know so little about
him.

CYNTHIA: Right Simon, it's your opening on the minor
bid. Hmm. Let's see. I think I'll overbid the spade
convention with two no trumps and King's gambit
offered there—(*discards*) and West's dummy split
double to Queen's Bishop 4 there!

MAGNUS (*as he plays cards*): Faites vos jeux. Rien ne
va plus. Rouge et noir. Zéro.

CYNTHIA: Simon?

BIRDBOOT (*triumphant, leaping to his feet*): And I call
your bluff!

CYNTHIA (*imperturbably*): I meld.

FELICITY: I huff.

MAGNUS: I ruff.

BIRDBOOT: I bluff.

CYNTHIA: Twist.

FELICITY: Bust.

MAGNUS: Check.

BIRDBOOT: Snap.

CYNTHIA: How's that?

FELICITY: Not out.

MAGNUS: Double top.

BIRDBOOT: Bingo!

Climax.

CYNTHIA: No! Simon—your luck's in tonight.

FELICITY: We shall see—the night is not over yet, Simon
Gascoyne! (*She exits quickly.*)

BIRDBOOT (*looking after* FELICITY): Red herring—smell

it a mile off. (*To* MAGNUS.) Oh yes, she's as clean as a whistle, I've seen it a thousand times. And I've seen you before too, haven't I? Strange—there's something about you . . .

MAGNUS: Care for a spin round the rose garden, Cynthia?

CYNTHIA: No Magnus, I must talk to Simon.

BIRDBOOT: There's nothing for you there, you know.

MAGNUS: You think so?

BIRDBOOT: Oh yes, she knows which side her bread is buttered. I am a man not without a certain influence among those who would reap the limelight—she's not going to throw me over for a heavily disguised cripple.

MAGNUS: There's an old Canadian proverb—

BIRDBOOT: Don't give me that—I tumbled to you right from the start—oh yes, you chaps are not as clever as you think. . . . Sooner or later you make your mistake. . . . Incidentally, where was it I saw you? . . . I've definitely. . . .

CYNTHIA (*calling*): Simon!

MAGNUS (*leaving*): Well, I think I'll go and oil my gun. (*Exit.*)

BIRDBOOT (*after* MAGNUS): Double bluff!—(*To* CYNTHIA.) I've seen it a thousand times.

CYNTHIA: I think Magnus suspects something. And Felicity . . . Simon, was there anything between you and Felicity?

BIRDBOOT: No, no—that's all over now. I merely flattered her a little over a drink, told her she'd go far, that sort of thing. Dear me, the fuss that's been made over a simple flirtation—

CYNTHIA (*as* MRS. DRUDGE *enters behind*): If I find you

51

have falsely seduced me from my dear husband Albert, I will kill you, Simon Gascoyne!

The "Curtain" as before. MRS. DRUDGE *and* CYNTHIA *leave.* BIRDBOOT *starts to follow them.*

MOON: *Birdboot!*

BIRDBOOT *stops.*

MOON: For God's sake pull yourself together.
BIRDBOOT: I can't help it.
MOON: What do you think you're doing? You're turning it into a complete farce!
BIRDBOOT: I know, I know—but I can't live without her. (*He is making erratic neurotic journeys about the stage.*) I shall resign my position, of course. I don't care I'm a goner, I tell you—(*He has arrived at the body. He looks at it in surprise, hesitates, bends and turns it over.*)

MOON: Birdboot, think of your family, your friends—your high standing in the world of letters—I say, what are you doing?

BIRDBOOT *is staring at the body's face.*

Birdboot . . . leave it alone. Come and sit down—what's the matter with you?

BIRDBOOT (*dead-voiced*): It's Higgs.
MOON: What?
BIRDBOOT: It's Higgs.

Pause.

MOON: Don't be silly.
BIRDBOOT: I tell you it's Higgs!

MOON *half-rises. Bewildered.*

52

I don't understand . . . He's dead.

MOON: Dead?

BIRDBOOT: Who would want to . . .

MOON: He must have been lying there all the time. . . .

BIRDBOOT: . . . kill Higgs?

MOON: But what's he doing here? I was standing in
tonight. . . .

BIRDBOOT (*turning*): Moon? . . .

MOON (*in wonder, quietly*): So it's me and Puckeridge
now.

BIRDBOOT: Moon . . . ?

MOON (*faltering*): But I swear I . . .

BIRDBOOT: I've got it—

MOON: But I didn't—

BIRDBOOT (*quietly*): My God . . . so that was it. . . .
(*Up.*) Moon—now I see—

MOON: —I swear I didn't—

BIRDBOOT: Now—finally—I see it all—

There is a shot and BIRDBOOT *falls dead.*

MOON: Birdboot! (*He runs on, to Birdboot's body.*)

CYNTHIA *appears at the French windows. She stops
and stares. All as before.*

CYNTHIA: Oh my God—what happened, Inspector?

MOON (*almost to himself*): He's dead. . . . (*He rises.*)
That's a bit rough, isn't it?—a bit extreme!—He may
have had his faults—I admit he was a fickle old . . .
Who did this, and why?

MOON *turns to face her. He stands up and makes
swiftly for his seat. Before he gets there he is
stopped by the sound of voices.* SIMON *and* HOUND
are occupying the critics' seats. MOON *freezes.*

53

SIMON: To say that it is without pace, point, focus, interest, drama, wit or originality is to say simply that it does not happen to be my cup of tea. One has only to compare this ragbag with the masters of the genre to see that here we have a trifle that is not my cup of tea at all.

HOUND: I'm sorry to be blunt but there is no getting away from it. It lacks pace. A complete ragbag.

SIMON: I will go further. Those of you who were fortunate enough to be at the Comédie-Française on Wednesday last, will not need to be reminded that hysterics are no substitute for *éclat*.

HOUND: It lacks *élan*.

SIMON: Some of the cast seem to have given up acting altogether, apparently aghast, with every reason, at finding themselves involved in an evening that would, and indeed will, make the angels weep.

HOUND: I am not a prude but I fail to see any reason for the shower of filth and sexual allusion foisted onto an unsuspected public in the guise of modernity at all costs. . . .

Behind MOON, FELICITY, MAGNUS *and* MRS. DRUDGE *have made their entrances, so that he turns to face their semicircle.*

MAGNUS (*pointing to Birdboot's body*): Well, Inspector, is this your man?

MOON (*warily*): . . . Yes. . . . Yes. . . .

CYNTHIA: It's Simon . . .

MOON: Yes . . . yes . . . poor. . . . (*Up*) Is this some kind of a joke?

MAGNUS: If it is, Inspector, it's in very poor taste.

54

MOON *pulls himself together and becomes galvanic, a little wild, in grief for* BIRDBOOT.

MOON: All right! I'm going to find out who did this! I want everyone to go to the positions they occupied when the shot was fired—

They move; hysterically.

No one will leave the house!

• They move back.

MAGNUS: I think we all had the opportunity to fire the shot, Inspector—
MOON (*furious*): I am not—
MAGNUS: —but which of us would want to?
MOON: Perhaps you, Major Magnus!
MAGNUS: Why should I want to kill him?
MOON: Because he was on to you—yes, he tumbled you right from the start—and you shot him just when he was about to reveal that you killed—(MOON *points, pauses and then crosses to Higgs' body and falters*)—killed—(*he turns* HIGGS *over*) . . . this . . . chap.
MAGNUS: But what motive would there be for killing him? (*Pause.*) Who *is* this chap? (*Pause.*) Inspector?
MOON (*rising*): I don't know. Quite unlike anyone I've ever met. (*Long pause.*) Well . . . now . . .
MRS. DRUDGE: Inspector?
MOON (*eagerly*): Yes? Yes, what is it, dear lady?
MRS. DRUDGE: Happening to enter this room earlier in the day to close the windows, I chanced to overhear a remark made by the deceased Simon Gas-

coyne to her ladyship, viz., "I will kill anyone who comes between us."

MOON: Ah—yes—well, that's it, then. This . . . chap . . . (*pointing to the body*) was obviously killed by (*pointing to Birdboot's body*) er . . . (*the moment of Moon's betrayal, for which he is to pay with his life*) . . . by (*pause*) Simon.

CYNTHIA: But he didn't come between us!

MAGNUS: And who, then, killed Simon?

MRS. DRUDGE: Subsequent to that reported remark, I also happened to be in earshot of a remark made by Lady Muldoon to the deceased, to the effect, "I will kill you, Simon Gascoyne!" I hope you don't mind my mentioning it.

MOON: Not at all. I'm glad you did. It is from these chance remarks that we in the Force build up our complete picture before moving in to make the arrest. It will not be long now, I fancy, and I must warn you, Lady Muldoon that anything you say—

CYNTHIA: Yes!—I hated Simon Gascoyne, for he had me in his thrall!—But I didn't kill him!

MRS. DRUDGE: Prior to that, Inspector, I also chanced to overhear a remark made by Miss Cunningham, no doubt in the heat of the moment, but it stuck in my mind as these things do, viz., "I will kill you for this, Simon Gascoyne!"

MOON: Ah! The final piece of the jigsaw! I think I am now in a position to reveal the mystery. This man (*the corpse*) was, of course, McCoy, the Canadian who, as we heard, meeting Gascoyne in the street and being solicited for sixpence for a toffee apple, smacked him across the ear, with the cry, "How's that for a grudge to harbour, you sniffling little workshy!" all those many years ago. Gascoyne bided his time, but in due course tracked McCoy down to this house, having, on the way, met, in the neighbourhood, a simple ambitious girl from the provinces. He was charming, persuasive—told her, I have no doubt, that she would go straight to the top—and she, flattered by his sophistication, taken in by his promises to see her all right on the night, gave in to his simple desires. Perhaps she loved him. We shall never know. But in the very hour of her promised triumph, his eye fell on another—yes, I refer to Lady Cynthia Muldoon. From the moment he caught sight of her there was no other woman for him—he was in her spell, willing to sacrifice anything, even you, Felicity Cunningham. It was only today—unexpectedly finding him here—that you learned the truth. There was a bitter argument which ended with your promise to kill him—a promise that you carried out in this very room at your first opportunity! And I must warn you that anything you say—

FELICITY: But it doesn't make sense!

MOON: Not at first glance, *perhaps*.

MAGNUS: Could not McCoy have been killed by the same person who killed Simon?

FELICITY: But why should any of us want to kill a perfect stranger?

MAGNUS: Perhaps he was not a stranger to *one* of us.

MOON (*faltering*): But Simon was the madman, wasn't he?

MAGNUS: We only have your word for that, Inspector. We only have your word for a lot of things. For instance—McCoy. Who is he? Is his name McCoy? Is there any truth in that fantastic and implausible tale of the insult inflicted in the Canadian streets? Or is there something else, something quite unknown to us, behind all this? Suppose for a moment that the madman, having killed this unknown stranger for private and inscrutable reasons of his own, was disturbed before he could dispose of the body, so having cut the telephone wires he decided to return to the scene of the crime, masquerading as—Police Inspector Hound!

MOON: But . . . I'm not mad . . . I'm almost sure I'm not mad . . .

MAGNUS: . . . only to discover that in the house was a man, Simon Gascoyne, who recognized the corpse as a man against whom you had held a deep-seated grudge—!

MOON: But I didn't kill—I'm almost sure I—

MAGNUS: I put it to you!—are you the real Inspector Hound?!

MOON: You know damn well I'm not! What's it all about?

MAGNUS: I thought as much.

MOON: I only dreamed . . . sometimes I dreamed—

CYNTHIA: So it was you!

MRS. DRUDGE: The madman!

FELICITY: The killer!

CYNTHIA: Oh, it's horrible, horrible.

MRS. DRUDGE: The stranger in our midst!

MAGNUS: Yes, we had a shrewd suspicion he would turn up here—and he walked into the trap!

MOON: What *trap?*

MAGNUS: I am not the real Magnus Muldoon—It was a mere subterfuge!—and (*standing up and removing*

58

his moustaches) I now reveal myself as—

CYNTHIA: You mean—?

MAGNUS:Yes! I am the real Inspector Hound!

MOON (*pause*): *Puckeridge!*

MAGNUS (*with pistol*): Stand where you are, or I shoot!

MOON (*backing*): Puckeridge! You killed Higgs—and Birdboot tried to tell me—

MAGNUS: Stop in the name of the law!

> MOON *turns to run.* MAGNUS *fires.* MOON *drops to his knees.*

I have waited a long time for this moment.

CYNTHIA: So you are the real Inspector Hound.

MAGNUS: Not only that!—I have been leading a double life—at *least!*

CYNTHIA: You mean—?

MAGNUS: Yes!—It's been ten long years, but don't you know me?

CYNTHIA: You mean—?

MAGNUS: Yes!—it is me, Albert!—who lost his memory and joined the Force, rising by merit to the rank of Inspector, his past blotted out—until fate cast him back into the home he left behind, back to the beautiful woman he had brought here as his girlish bride—in short, my darling, my memory has returned and your long wait is over!

CYNTHIA: Oh, Albert!

> *They embrace.*

MOON (*with a trace of admiration*): Puckeridge! . . . you cunning bastard. (*He dies.*)

THE END

Selected List of Grove Press Drama and Theater Paperbacks

E312 ARDEN, JOHN / Serjeant Musgrave's Dance / $2.45
[See also Modern British Drama, Henry Popkin, ed. GT614 / $5.95]

B109 ARDEN, JOHN / Three Plays: Live Like Pigs, The Waters of Babylon, The Happy Haven / $2.45

E127 ARTAUD, ANTONIN / The Theater and Its Double (Critical Study) / $2.95

E425 BARAKA, IMAMU AMIRI (LEROI JONES) / The Baptism and The Toilet / $2.45

E540 BARNES, PETER / The Ruling Class / $2.95

E471 BECKETT, SAMUEL / Cascando and Other Short Dramatic Pieces (Words and Music, Film, Play, Come and Go, Eh Joe, Endgame) / $1.95

E96 BECKETT, SAMUEL / Endgame / $1.95

E318 BECKETT, SAMUEL / Happy Days / $2.45

E226 BECKETT, SAMUEL / Krapp's Last Tape, plus All That Fall, Embers, Act Without Words I and II / $2.45

E33 BECKETT, SAMUEL / Waiting For Godot / $1.95 [See also Seven Plays of the Modern Theater, Harold Clurman, ed. GT422 / $4.95]

B79 BEHAN, BRENDAN / The Quare Fellow* and The Hostage**: Two Plays / $2.45 *[See also Seven Plays of the Modern Theater, Harold Clurman, ed. GT422 / $4.95] **[See also Modern British Drama, Henry Popkin, ed. GT614 / $5.95]

B117 BRECHT, BERTOLT / The Good Woman of Setzuan / $1.95

B80 BRECHT, BERTOLT / The Jewish Wife and Other Short Plays (In Search of Justice, The Informer, The Elephant Calf, The Measures Taken, The Exception and the Rule, Salzburg Dance of Death) / $1.65

B90 BRECHT, BERTOLT / The Mother / $1.45

B108 BRECHT, BERTOLT / Mother Courage and Her Children / $1.50

B333 BRECHT, BERTOLT / The Threepenny Opera / $1.45

B88 BRECHT, BERTOLT / The Visions of Simone Machard / $1.25

E259 IONESCO, EUGENE / Rhinoceros* and Other Plays (The Leader, The Future is in Eggs, or It Takes All Sorts to Make a World) / $1.95 *[See also Seven Plays of the Modern Theater, Harold Clurman, ed. GT422 / $4.95]

E485 IONESCO, EUGENE / A Stroll in the Air and Frenzy for Two: Two Plays / $2.45

E119 IONESCO, EUGENE / Three Plays (Amédée, The New Tenant, Victims of Duty) / $2.95

E387 IONESCO, EUGENE / Notes and Counter Notes / $3.95

E633 LAHR, JOHN (Ed.) / Grove Press Modern Drama / $6.95 (The Caucasian Chalk Circle by Bertolt Brecht, The Toilet by Imamu Amiri Baraka (LeRoi Jones), The White House Murder Case by Jules Feiffer, The Blacks by Jean Genet, Rhinoceros by Eugene Ionesco, Tango by Slawomir Mrozek)

E433 MROZEK, SLAWOMIR / Tango / $1.95

E462 NICHOLS, PETER / Joe Egg / $2.95

E567 ORTON, JOE / What The Butler Saw / $2.40

E583 OSBORNE, JOHN / Inadmissible Evidence / $2.45

B354 PINTER, HAROLD / Old Times / $1.95

E315 PINTER, HAROLD / The Birthday Party* and The Room: Two Plays / $1.95 *[See also Seven Plays of the Modern Theater, Harold Clurman, ed. GT422 / $4.95]

E299 PINTER, HAROLD / The Caretaker* and The Dumb Waiter: Two Plays / $1.95 *[See also Modern British Drama, Henry Popkin, ed. GT422 / $5.95]

E411 PINTER, HAROLD / The Homecoming / $1.95

E432 PINTER, HAROLD / The Lover, Tea Party, The Basement: Three Plays / $1.95

E480 PINTER, HAROLD / A Night Out, Night School, Revue Sketches: Early Plays / $1.95

GT614 POPKIN, HENRY (Ed.) / Modern British Drama / $5.95 (A Taste of Honey by Shelagh Delaney, The Hostage by Brendan Behan, Roots by Arnold Wesker, Serjeant Musgrave's Dance by John Arden, One Way Pendulum by N. F. Simpson, The Caretaker by Harold Pinter)

E635 SHEPARD, SAM / The Tooth of Crime and Geography of a Horsedreamer / $3.95

E626 STOPPARD, TOM / Jumpers / $1.95

B319 STOPPARD, TOM / Rosencrantz and Guilderstern Are Dead / $1.95

E660 STOREY, DAVID / In Celebration / $2.95